A Note to Parents and Teachers

Eyewitness Readers is a compelling new reading programme for children. *Eyewitness* has become the most trusted name in illustrated books, and this new series combines the highly visual *Eyewitness* approach with engaging, easy-to-read stories. Each *Eyewitness Reader* is guaranteed to capture a child's interest while developing his or her reading skills, general knowledge, and love of reading.

The books are written by leading children's authors and are designed in conjunction with literacy experts, including Cliff Moon M.Ed., Honorary Fellow of the University of Reading. Cliff Moon spent many years as a teacher and teacher educator specializing in reading. He has written more than 140 books for children and teachers and he reviews regularly for teachers' journals.

The four levels of *Eyewitness Readers* are aimed at different reading abilities, enabling you to choose the books that are exactly right for each child:

Level One–Beginning to read
Level Two–Beginning to read alone
Level Three–Reading alone
Level Four–Proficient readers

The "normal" age at which a child begins to read can be anywhere from three to eight years old, so these levels are only general guidelines.

No matter which level you select, you can be sure that you're helping children learn to read, then read to learn!

www.dk.com

Created by Leapfrog Press Ltd

Project Editor Naia Bray-Moffatt
Art Editor Jane Horne

For Dorling Kindersley
Senior Editor Mary Atkinson
Managing Art Editor Peter Bailey
Production Melanie Dowland
Picture Researcher Liz Moore

Natural History Consultant
Theresa Greenaway

Reading Consultant
Cliff Moon M.Ed.

Published in Great Brtain by
Dorling Kindersley Limited
9 Henrietta Street
London WC2E 8PS

2 4 6 8 10 9 7 5 3 1

Eyewitness Readers™ is a trademark of
Dorling Kindersley Limited, London.

A CIP catalogue record for this book is
available from the British Library.

ISBN 0 7513-6211-5

Colour reproduction by Colourscan, Singapore
Printed and bound in Belgium by Proost

The publisher would like to thank the following
for their kind permission to reproduce their photographs:
t=top, a=above, b=below, l=left, r=right, c=centre
Bruce Coleman Collection: 6br, 10-11t, 10b, 12cl, cb, lb,
17t, 23br, 27t, b, 32cr, br, 33; Dorling Kindersley Picture Library/
Natural History Museum: 22bl, 28cl, cr, br; Empics: 8br; NHPA: 28;
Pictor International Ltd: 15br, bl, cr, cl, 26b, 30b, 31;
Telegraph Colour Library: 4-5, 16, 19t.
Additional photography by: Geoff Brightling, Jane Burton,
Peter Chadwick, Andy Crawford, Steve Gorton, Frank Greenaway,
Dave King, Karl Shone, James Stevenson, Kim Taylor.
Modelmakers: Peter Griffiths, Peter Minster/Model FX,
Chris Reynolds and the BBC Team.
Additional design: Adrienne Hutchinson, Catherine Goldsmith.

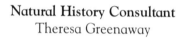

EYEWITNESS READERS

BEGINNING TO READ ALONE 2

The Secret Life of Trees

Written by Chiara Chevallier

London • New York • Sydney • Delhi

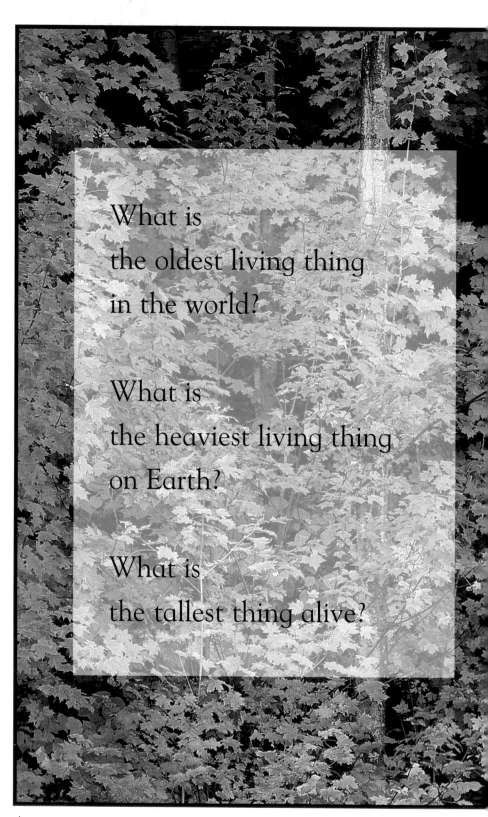

What is
the oldest living thing
in the world?

What is
the heaviest living thing
on Earth?

What is
the tallest thing alive?

The answer
to all three questions
is . . . a tree!

Trees are all around us.
But what do you
really know about them?

Turn the page and discover
the secret world of trees.

When you look at a tree
what do you see?

You see bark that protects
the tree's trunk and branches.
The bark at the bottom is old.
It is rough and cracked.
The bark at the top
is young and smooth.

The tallest tree
The tallest tree alive today is
over 150 metres high! It is a coast
redwood growing in California.
There is enough wood in its
trunk to build over 300 houses!

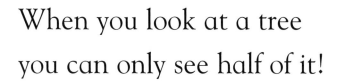

When you look at a tree
you can only see half of it!

The other half is underground.
These are the roots,
pushing their way through
the thick earth.

Rooting around
The roots of a tree
150 metres tall, take
up the same space
under the earth as
a football pitch!

Roots can spread out
through the soil as far
as the tree is high.

A tree can live longer
than all other living things.
It may live for hundreds –
even thousands – of years!

The oldest tree

The oldest recorded
tree in the world
is a bristlecone pine.
It is an amazing
4,900 years old.

A tree needs sunlight and
water to grow.

High above the ground,
the tree's leaves use energy
from the sun to make food.
Below ground, the tree's roots
spread out in search of water.

When you look at a tree you can see
a home for many animals and birds.

High up in the branches,
birds carefully build nests.
They lay their eggs out of sight
and out of reach of other animals.

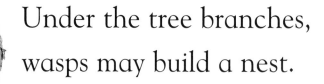

Under the tree branches,
wasps may build a nest.

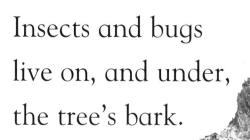

Insects and bugs
live on, and under,
the tree's bark.

Insect disguise
Some insects, like these thorn bugs, disguise themselves as part of a tree so they don't get eaten.

In the earth,
under the roots of a tree,
rabbits and badgers
dig their homes.

A tree in summer is an animal hotel!

Trees come in all shapes and sizes, but there are two main types:

broad-leaved trees

and conifers.

A broad-leaved tree has large, flat leaves on its wide-spreading branches.

The shady green forests
of Europe are mostly made up
of broad-leaved trees.

Many broad-leaved trees
change their leaves
as the seasons change.

In the cold chill of winter,
most broad-leaved trees
have no leaves.
The leaves have fallen off
because there is less sunlight.

As spring begins,
fresh new leaves open
from buds on the branches.
The tree wakes up
from its winter sleep
as the days get longer
and there is more sunlight.

By summer, the tree is covered
with bright, green leaves.
Its leaves give shade,
shelter and food
to many animals and insects.

In the misty autumn,
as the weather gets colder,
the tree's leaves change colour.
Some leaves turn brown.
Others turn bright yellow
or brilliant red.
Then they fall
to the ground.
The tree is getting ready
to sleep again until next spring.

New trees are born
when older trees
drop their seeds
on the ground.

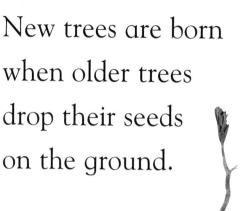

A seed faces
many dangers.
Hungry animals
may eat it.

It may be stepped on and crushed.

Most seeds never survive

to grow into a tree.

Broad-leaved trees protect their seeds.

Some put them in a hard shell

like an acorn or a chestnut.

Not all trees
lose their leaves
in winter.
Some are evergreen
like conifers.

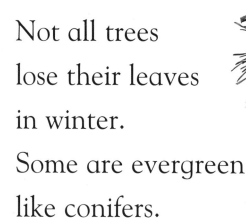

Conifers can live in colder places
than most broad-leaved trees.
Instead of wide, flat leaves,
they have short, sharp needles
that snow slides off easily.

Bouncy branches

The branches of a conifer
are bouncy, so they don't
snap even when they are
covered with thick snow.

Conifer trees
produce hard,
scaly cones
to protect their seeds.

Cones come in different sizes.
The smallest is only 1 cm long
but the cone of the
sugar pine is 60 cm long.

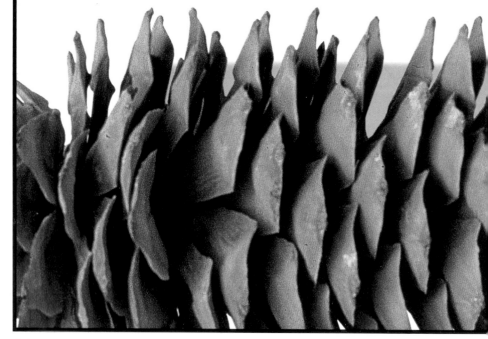

A pine cone can help you
forecast the weather!
When it is warm,
the scales of the cone
open up.
They close again when
a storm is on the way
so that the seeds
are kept dry.

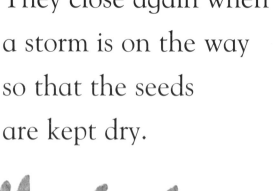

Wherever you are in the world
you can usually find
trees growing.

In the steamy, wet jungles,
trees grow so close together
that hardly any light
reaches the forest floor.

Thanks to the heat and rainfall,
these trees grow faster
than other trees –
up to three metres each year.

Tree houses

In the African forests,
chimpanzees spend nearly
all their lives up in the trees.
They only go down to the
jungle floor to look for food.

Tropical trees grow
in the warmest countries
of the world.
Lots of tasty fruits and nuts
come from tropical trees:
avocados, dates,
mangoes and Brazil nuts.

Coconut palms grow wild
on the beaches of
many tropical countries.
This palm tree's seed
is inside its hairy
coconut.
It contains milk so that
the seed can start growing
even if it is washed up
on very dry land.

Killer trees
The seed of the strangler fig
grows in the roots of another
tree. The fig's roots strangle the
tree and cut out the sunlight
until the other tree dies.

When you look at a tree
you can see where
wood and paper come from.

The table you sit at
and the chair
you sit on
may be made
of wood.

The swing
you play on
may be made
of wood.

And the biggest secret of all?
Even the book you are reading
comes from a tree!

Identifying Trees

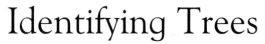

The easiest way to identify a broad-leaved tree is to look at the leaves. The leaves of each type of tree have their own size and shape. Here are the leaves of common trees you might see.

Lime The leaves are heart-shaped with a jagged edge and have long stems. These trees are popular in large gardens.

Ash These feather-like leaves have from three to thirteen leaflets, with the odd one at the end. Ash trees are often planted at the sides of streets.

Horse chestnut The leaves have seven or nine leaflets that point outwards like a hand. You might see these trees growing in parks or along streets.

Oak There are many types of oak tree but most have toothed leaves, like this English Oak leaf. They are often found in woods.

Maple Most types of maple leaf are easy to recognize by their hand-like shape. In the autumn, the leaves often turn a fiery red.

Holly The holly is evergreen so even in winter you will find these prickly, shiny green leaves.